# Barber Shop Songs

*The 83 songs in this collection can be sung by any quartet or four part chorus, male or mixed. The melody will be found in the upper part except where it is indicated. Guitar frames have been added to those songs where the guitar would blend effectively with the voices.*

Order No. AM 40270
International Standard Book Number: 0.8256.2067.8

*Exclusive Distributors:*
Music Sales Corporation
257 Park Avenue South, New York, NY 10010 USA
Music Sales Limited
8/9 Frith Street, London W1V 5TZ England
Music Sales Pty. Limited
120 Rothschild Street, Rosebery, Sydney NSW 2018, Australia

Printed in the United States of America by
Vicks Lithograph and Printing Corporation

**Amsco Publications**
New York/London/Sydney

# ALPHABETICAL INDEX

# CLASSIFIED INDEX

# Pal Of My Dreams

## (Waltz Ballad)

CHARLES E. ROAT
*Arr.* R.J.N.

**Moderately slow**

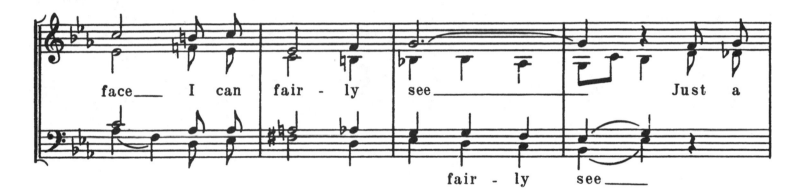

CHORUS

Dear old pal, how I miss you, I'm lone - ly to - night_ Dear old

pal just to kiss you would make things seem right_ For the

sweet - est of mem - o - ries come back to me___ I am

long - ing to hold you a - gain ten - der - ly___ Ev - 'ry

star in the night brings your mes - sage of love, And it's

far shi - ning light tells me you're up a - bove.___

I hear you call - ing to me now it seems___

Oh how I miss you___ Pal of my dreams.

Pal___ of my dreams.

2. How my heart seems to yearn
   And my thoughts ever turn
   To those days of the long ago
   All the world I would give
   If once more I could live
   O'er the years that you loved me so.

# She Is More To Be Pitied Than Censured

WILLIAM M. GRAY
*Arr.* R.J.N.

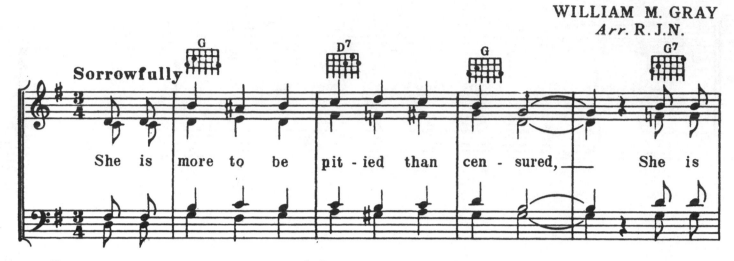

She is more to be pit-ied than cen-sured,___ She is

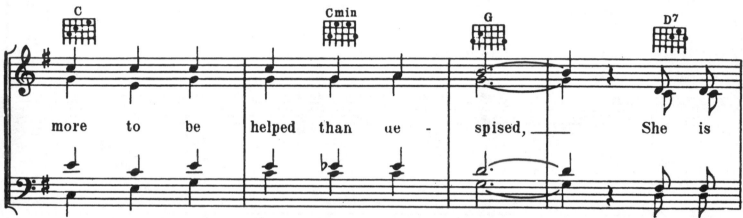

more to be helped than de-spised,___ She is

on-ly a las sie who ven-tured,___ On

life's storm-y path, ill ad-vised,___ Do not

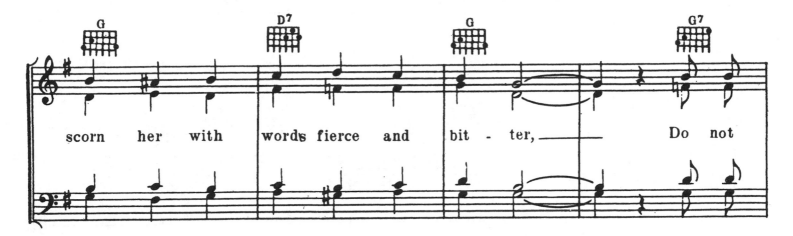

scorn her with words fierce and bit - ter, ____ Do not

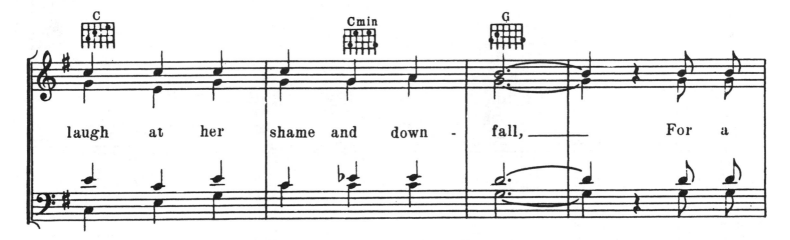

laugh at her shame and down - fall, ____ For a

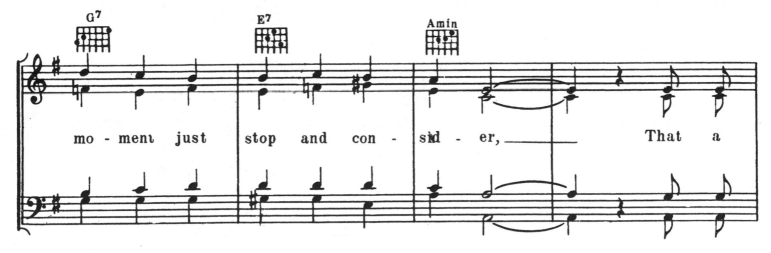

mo - ment just stop and con - sid - er, ____ That a

man was the cause of it all. ____

# I Had A Dream, Dear

CHARLES N. DANIELS
*Arr.* R. J. N.

# She May Have Seen Better Days

JAMES THORNTON
Arr. R.J.N.

**Moderately fast**

1. While stroll-ing a - long with the ci-ty's vast throng, On a night that was

oit - ter - ly cold, (so___ cold) I___ no - ticed a crowd who were

laugh-ing a - loud, At some-thing they chanced to be-hold, (to be -

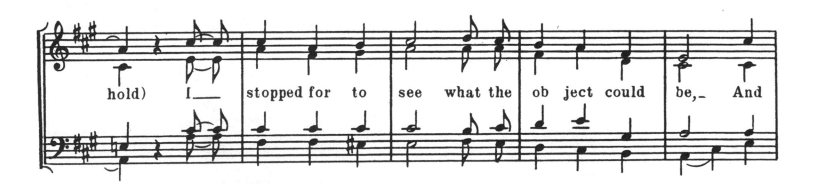

hold) I___ stopped for to see what the ob ject could be,___ And

there on a door-step lay,(door-step lay) A wo-man in tears, from the

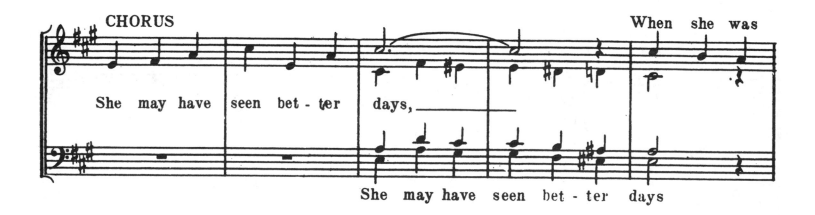

crowd's an-gry jeers, And then I heard some-bod-y say:(some-bod-y say)

**CHORUS**

When she was

She may have seen bet-ter days,_____

She may have seen bet-ter days

in her prime;

She may have seen bet-ter

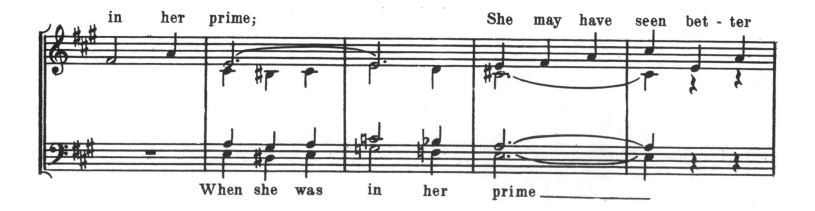

When she was in her prime_____

days, _____ Once up-on a time. _____

She may have seen bet-ter days up-on a time, once up-on __ a

Tho' by the way-side she fell She may

time. _____ Tho' by the way-side she fell, _____

yet mend her ways. Some poor old moth-er is

mend her ways. _____

wait-ing for her Who has seen bet-ter days. _____

wait-ing for her Who has seen bet-ter days, She's seen bet-ter days.

2. If we could but tell why the poor creature fell,
Perhaps we'd be not so severe;
If the truth were but known of this outcast alone,
Mayhap we would all shed a tear.
She was once someone's joy, cast aside like a toy,
Abandoned, forsaken, unknown.
Ev'ry man standing by, had a tear in his eye,
For some had a daughter at home.

3 The crowd went away, but I longer did stay;
For from her I was loathe to depart.
I knew by her moan, as she sat there alone,
That something was breaking her heart.
She told me her life, she was once a good wife,
Respected and honored by all;
Her husband had fled ere they were long wed,
And tears down her cheeks sadly fall.

# Come Home, Father!

HENRY C. WORK
*Arr.* R.J.N.

Moderately slow

1. Fa - ther, dear fa - ther, come home with me now! The clock in the stee - ple strikes one, _____ You steeple strikes one said you were com - ing right home from the shop, As soon as your days work was done, _____ Our fire has gone out, our

house is all dark, And moth-er's been watch-ing since

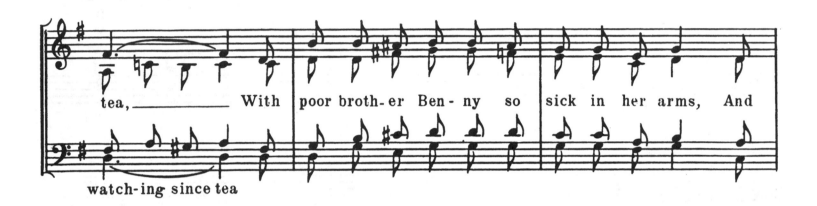

tea,_____ With poor broth-er Ben-ny so sick in her arms, And

watch-ing since tea

no one to help her but me._____ Come home! come home! come

home!___ Please fa-ther, dear fa-ther, come home.___

CHORUS

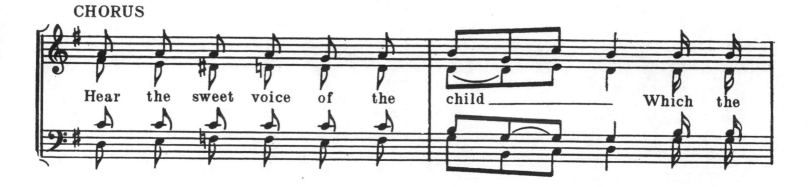

Hear the sweet voice of the child _____ Which the

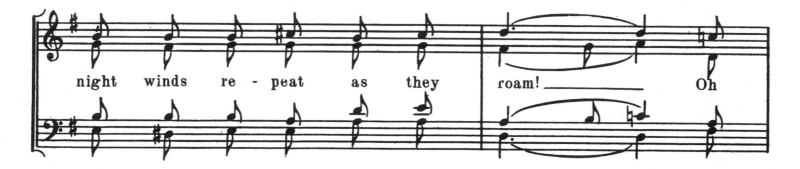

night winds re - peat as they roam! _____ Oh

who could re - sist this most plain - tive of pray'rs, "Please,__

fa - ther, dear__ fa - ther, come home!"____

2. Father, dear father, come home with me now!
The clock in the steeple strikes two;
The night has grown colder and Benny is worse,
But he has been calling for you.
Indeed he is worse, Ma says he will die,
Perhaps before morning shall dawn;
And this is the message she sent me to bring,
"Come quickly or he will be gone."
Come home! come home! come home!
*Please*, father, *dear* father, come home.

3. Father, dear father, come home with me now!
The clock in the steeple strikes three;
The night is so lonely, the hours are so long,
For poor weeping mother and me.
Yes, we are alone, poor Benny is dead,
And gone with the angels of light;
And these were the very last words that he said,
"I want to kiss Papa goodnight."
Come home! come home! come home!
*Please*, father, *dear* father, come home.

# Daisies Won't Tell

ANITA OWEN
*Arr.* R.J.N.

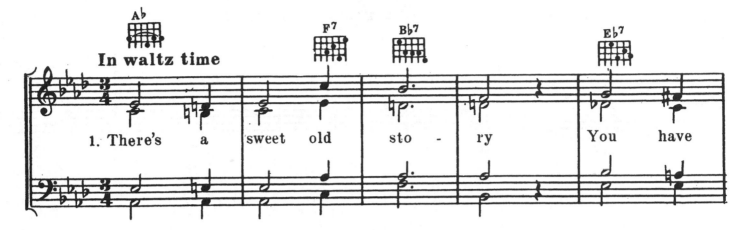

In waltz time

1. There's a sweet old sto - ry You have

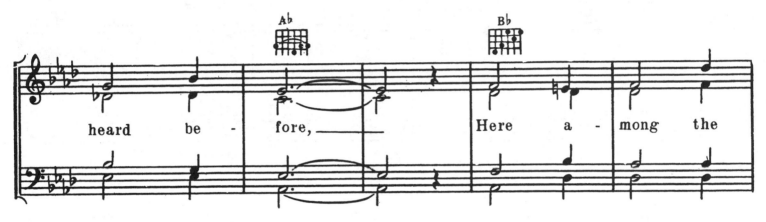

heard be - fore, Here a - mong the

dai - sies Let me tell it o'er;

On - ly say you love me, For I love you

well, ____ An - swer with a kiss,

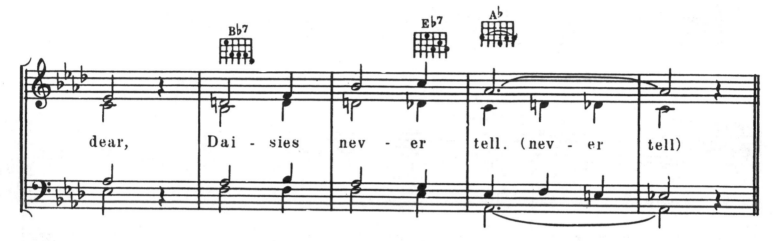

dear, Dai - sies nev - er tell. (nev - er tell)

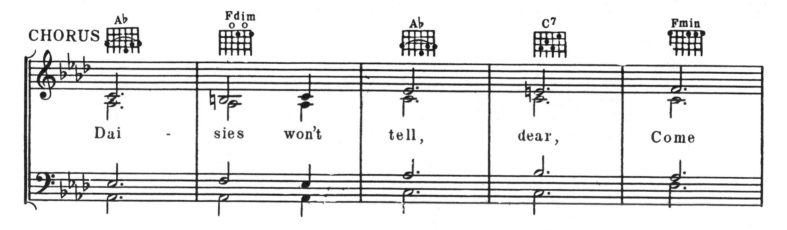

CHORUS Dai - sies won't tell, dear, Come

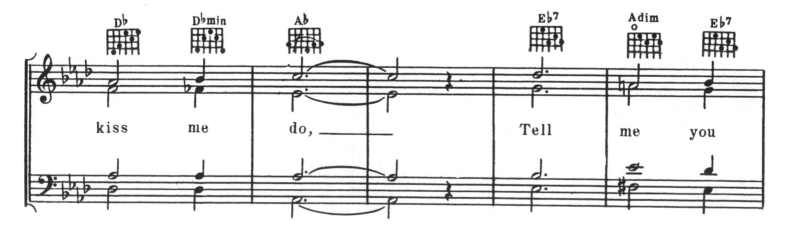

kiss me do, ____ Tell me you

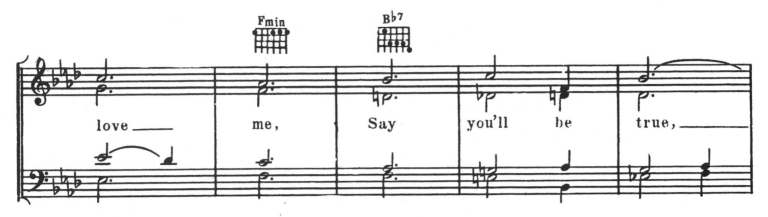

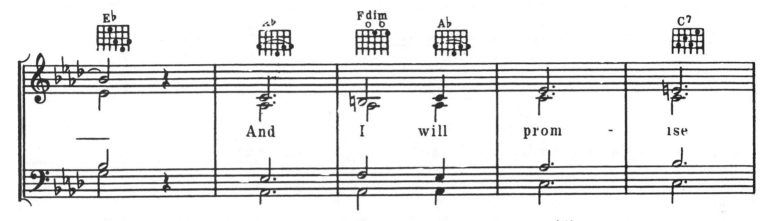

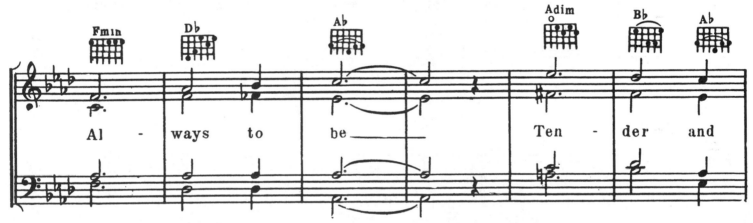

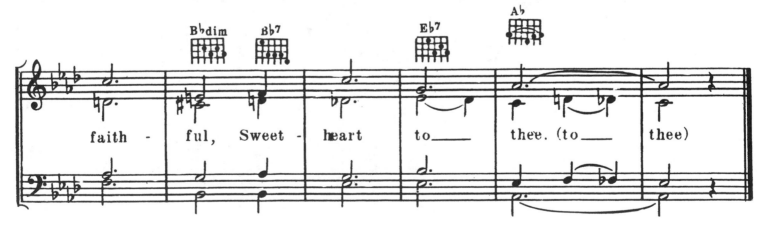

2. In a dream I fancied you were by my side.
While I gathered daisies one long chain you tied.
'Round us both I wound it, close I held you, too,
Daisies never tell, dear, make that dream come true.

# Always Take Mother's Advice

JENNIE LINDSAY
*Arr.* R.J.N.

you in the world she is dear-est,___ At your down-fall her grief is sev-

er - est!___ So don't cause her sor - row or pain.___

**CHORUS**

Al-ways take moth-er's ad-vice,___ She knows what is best for your good.___

Let her kind words then suf - fice, And al-ways take moth-er's ad-vice!___

2. Honor your mother so dear,
   You'll never know her worth till she's gone.
   Respect her grey hair while she's here,
   You'll grieve when she leaves you alone.
   On earth you will ne'er have another,
   In this weary world there's no other,
   And God only gives you one mother!
   So cherish and love her most dear.

# My Sweetheart's The Man In The Moon

JAMES THORNTON
*Arr.* R.J.N.

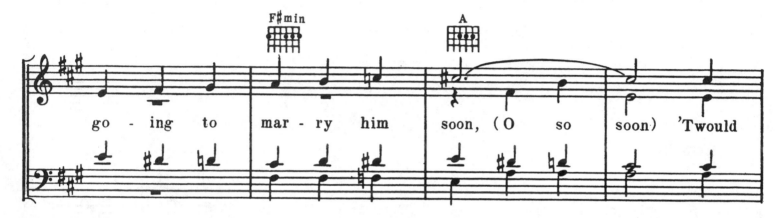

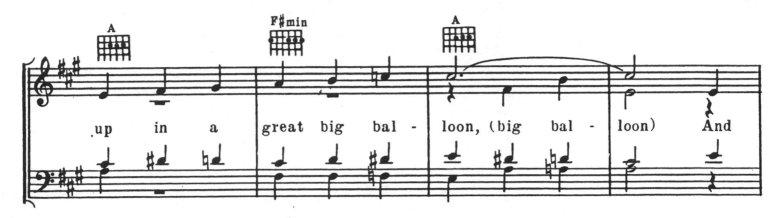

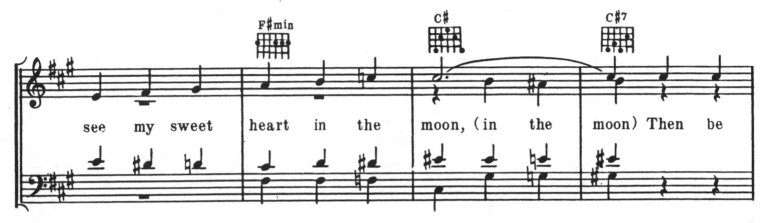

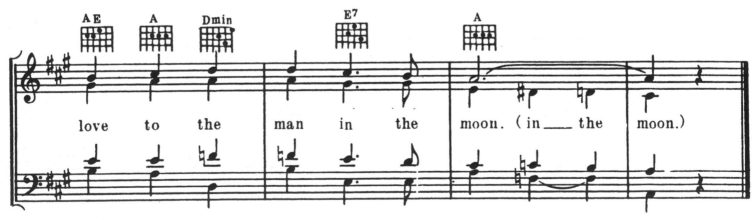

2. Last night while the stars brightly shone, he told me through Love's Telephone,
   That when we were wed, he'd go early to bed,
   And never stay out with the boys, so he said,
   We are going to marry next June, the wedding takes place in the moon,
   A sweet little Venus, we'll fondle between us,
   When I wed my old man in the moon.

# I've A Longing In My Heart For You, Louise

CHARLES K. HARRIS
*Arr.* R.J.N.

Slowly

I've a long-ing in my heart for you, Louise And for the dear old sun-ny south-ern home, _____ I can scent the hon-ey-suck-le and the fra-grant jess-a-mine, I've a long-ing in my heart for you, for you, for you.

# Little Annie Rooney

MICHAEL NOLAN
*Arr.* R.J.N.

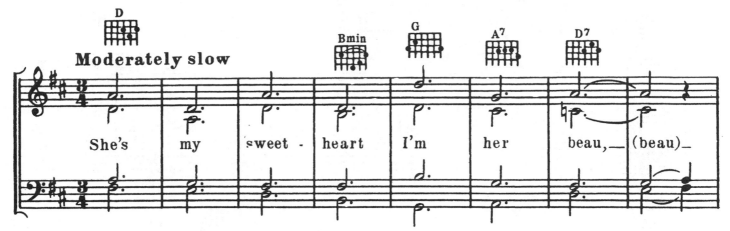

Moderately slow

She's my sweet - heart I'm her beau,__ (beau)__

She's my An - nie__ I'm her Joe.__

An - nie__

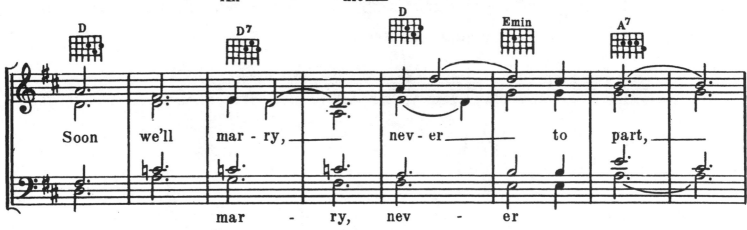

Soon we'll mar - ry,__ nev - er__ to part,__

mar - ry, nev - er

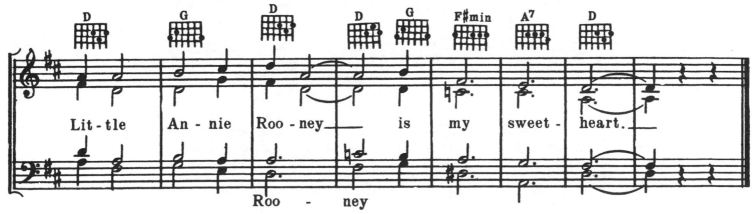

Lit - tle An - nie Roo - ney__ is my sweet - heart.

Roo - ney

# Clementine

P. MONTROSE
*Arr.* R.J.N.

2. Light she was and like a fairy, and her shoes were number nine;
   Herring boxes, without topses sandals were for Clementine.

3. Drove ducklings to the water, ev'ry morning just at nine,
   Hit her foot against a splinter, fell into the foaming brine.

4. Ruby lips above the water, blowing bubbles soft and fine;
   Alas for me! I was no swimmer, so I lost my Clementine.

# Sally In Our Alley

HENRY CAREY
*Arr.* R.J.N.

Slowly

1. Of all the girls that are so smart,— There's none like pret-ty Sal-ly; She is the dar-ling of my heart,— And lives in our Sal-ly, There is no la-dy in the land, That's half so sweet as al-ley Sal-ly; She is the dar-ling of my heart,— And lives in our al-ley. al-ley

2. Her father he makes cabbage nets
   And thro' the streets does cry 'em;
   Her mother she sells laces long
   To such as please to buy 'em;
   But sure such folks could ne'er beget,
   So sweet a girl as Sally;
   She is the darling of my heart
   And lives in our alley.

# There Is A Tavern In The Town

Old English Song
*Arr.* R. J. N.

1. There is a tav-ern in the town, in the town, And there my dear love sits him down, sits him down, And drinks his wine 'mid laugh-ter free, And nev-er, nev-er thinks of me.

CHORUS
Fare thee well for I must leave thee, Do not let the part-ing grieve thee, And re-
Oh fare thee well, Do not let the part-ing grieve thee, Re-

2. He left me for a damsel dark, damsel dark,
   Each Friday night they used to spark, used to spark,
   And now my love, once true to me,
   Takes that dark damsel on his knee.

3. Oh! dig my grave both wide and deep, wide and deep,
   Put tombstones at my head and feet, head and feet,
   And on my breast carve a turtle dove,
   To signify I died of love.

# I've Been Workin' On The Railroad

U.S. Southern Song
*Arr.* R. J. N.

blow - ing, \_\_\_\_ Rise up so ear - ly in the

morn, (in the morn) Oh don't you hear the cap - tain

shout - ing, \_\_\_\_ "Di - nah blow your horn."

# Billy Boy

EDWARD L. WHITE
*Arr.* R.J.N.

Lively

*Lead*

1. Oh\_\_\_ where\_ have you been. Bil - ly Boy,\_ Bill - ly

2. Did she bid you to come in, Billy Boy, Billy Boy,
Did she bid you to come in, charming Billy?
Yes, she bade me to come in, there's a dimple in her chin,
She's a young thing and cannot leave her mother.

3. Did she set for you a chair, Billy Boy, Billy Boy,
Did she set for you a chair, charming Billy?
Yes, she set for me a chair, she has ringlets in her hair,
She's a young thing and cannot leave her mother

# Sweet Marie

RAYMOND MOORE
*Arr. R.J.N.*

Why don't you come to me, Sweet Ma - rie, Sweet Ma -

rie, come to me, Not be - cause your face is fair, love, to see, (to see) But your

soul so pure and sweet, Makes my hap - pi - ness com - plete, Makes me

*Optional Ending*

fal - ter at your feet, Sweet Ma - rie. rie, Why don't you come, Sweet Ma - rie.

# Sweet and Low

JOSEPH BARNBY
*Arr.* R.J.N.

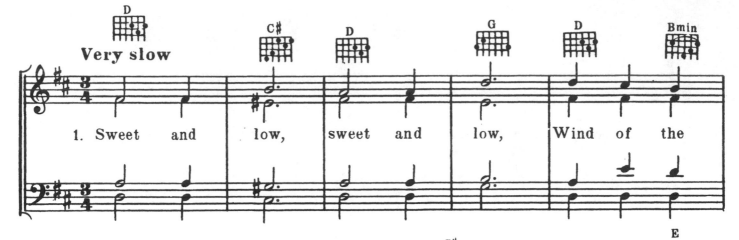

**Very slow**

1. Sweet and low, sweet and low, Wind of the

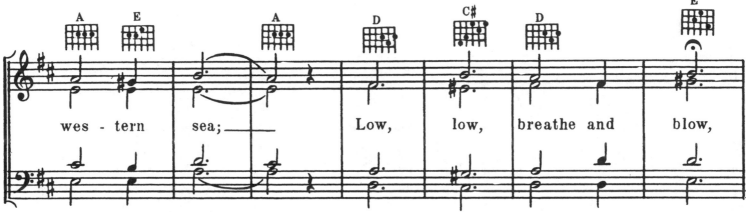

wes - tern sea; ___ Low, low, breathe and blow,

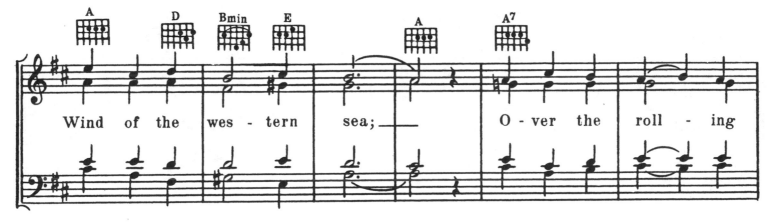

Wind of the wes - tern sea; ___ O - ver the roll - ing

wa - ters go, Come from the dy - ing moon ___ and

blow, Blow him a- gain to me, _____ While my

lit - tle one, while my pret- ty one sleeps. _____

2. Sleep and rest, sleep and rest, father will come to thee soon;
Rest, rest on mother's breast, father will come to thee soon;
Father will come to his babe in the nest,
Silver sails all out of the west,
Under the silver moon,
Sleep, my little one, sleep, my pretty one, sleep.

# Ben Bolt
## (Sweet Alice)

NELSON KNEASS
Arr. R.J.N.

**Moderately slow**

1. Oh! don't you re-mem- ber sweet Al- ice Ben Bolt, Sweet Al - ice with hair so

brown; She wept with de- light when you gave her a smile, And

2. Oh! don't you remember the wood Ben Bolt
   Near the green sunny slope of the hill
   When oft we have sung near it's wide spreading shade
   And kept time to the click of the mill.
   The mill has gone to decay Ben Bolt
   And a quiet now reigns all around
   See the old rustic porch with it's roses so sweet
   Lies scattered and fall'n to the ground
   See the old rustic porch with it's roses so sweet
   Lies scattered and falln to the ground.

# Barbara Allen

Old Scotch Song
*Arr.* R. J. N.

# Londonderry Air
## (Would God I Were The Tender Apple Blossom)

Irish Folk Song
*Arr.* R.J.N.

Very slowly

1. Would God I were the ten - der ap - ple

blos - som That floats and falls from off the twist - ed

bough, _____ To lie and faint with - in your silk - en

bo - som, With - in your silk - en bo - som as that does

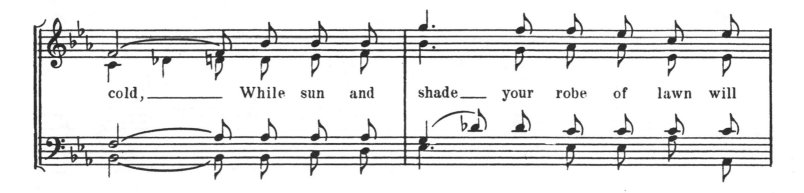

2. Yea, would to God that I were among the roses
   That lean to kiss you as you flow between,
   While on the lowest branch a bud uncloses,
   A bud uncloses to touch you, queen,
   Nay since you will not love, would I were growing,
   A happy daisy in the garden path,
   That so your silver foot might press me going,
   Might press me going even unto death.

# Seeing Nellie Home
## (The Quilting Party)

Old College Song
*Arr.* R. J. N.

On my arm a soft hand rested, rested light as ocean foam,
And 'twas from Aunt Dinah's quilting party I was seeing Nellie home.
I was seeing Nellie home, I was seeing Nellie home.
And 'twas from Aunt Dinah's quilting party I was seeing Nellie home.

# Drink To Me Only With Thine Eyes

Old English Melody
*Arr*. R.J.N.

1. Drink to me on-ly with thine eyes And I__ will pledge with mine, Or leave a kiss with-in__ the cup__ And I'll__ not ask for wine; The thirst that from the soul doth rise Doth ask a drink di-vine,__ Oh__ But might I of Jove's nec-tar sip__ I would not change for thine (not for__ thine)

2. I sent thee late a rosy wreath, not so much hon'ring thee,
   As giving it a hope that there it could not withered be;
   But thou thereon didst only breathe, and sent'st it back to me,
   Since when it grows and smells, I swear, not of itself but thee.

# The Band Played On

J. F. PALMER and
C. B. WARD
*Arr.* R.J.N.

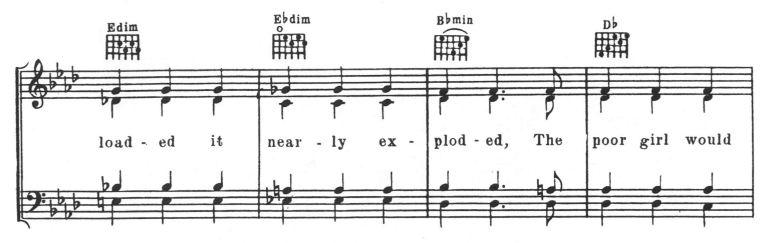

load - ed it near - ly ex - plod - ed, The poor girl would

shake with a - larm, (with a - larm) He'd ne'er leave the

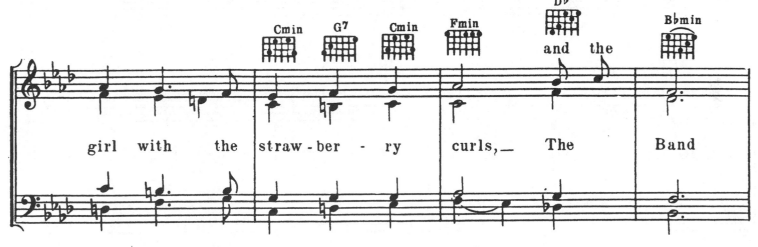

girl with the straw - ber - ry curls, __ The Band

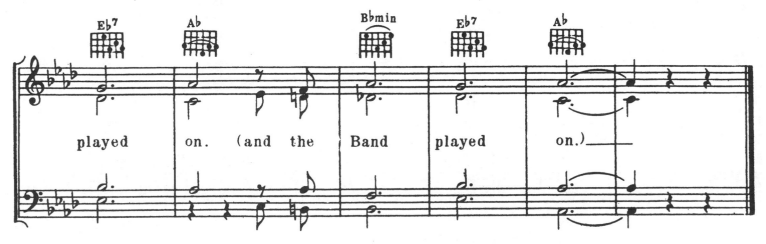

played on. (and the Band played on.) ____

# Juanita

Spanish Melody
*Arr.* R. J. N.

1. Soft oe'r the foun - tain, Ling -'ring falls the south - ern moon, Far o'er the moun - tain, Breaks the day too soon! In thy dark eyes' splen - dor, Where the warm light loves to dwell,

Wea - ry looks, yet ten - der, Speak their fond fare -

CHORUS

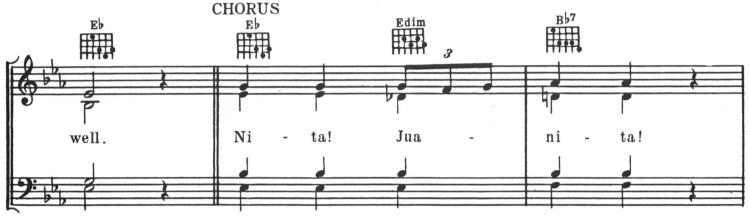

well. Ni - ta! Jua - ni - ta!

Ask thy soul if we should part, Ni - ta! Jua

ni - ta! Lean thee on my heart.

2. When in thy dreaming, moons like these shall shine again,
And daylight beaming, prove thy dreams are vain,
Wilt thou not, relenting, for thine absent lover sigh?
In thy heart consenting, to a prayer gone by.

# La Cucaracha

Mexican Song
*Arr.* R.J.N.

CHORUS

1. La Cu-ca-ra-cha, La Cu-ca-ra-cha, Heart and soul of Mex-i-co! La Cu-ca-
2. La Cu-ca-ra-cha, La Cu-ca-ra-cha, Lov-ers breathe it in a sigh! La Cu-ca-

(Hum_____)

ra-cha, La Cu-ca-ra-cha, Sing it high and sing it low! La Cu-ca-
ra-cha, La Cu-ca-ra-cha, Sol-diers sing it when they die! La Cu-ca-

ra-cha, La Cu-ca-ra-cha, Song of fight-ing and ro-mance! La Cu-ca-
ra-cha, La Cu-ca-ra-cha, For the brave and for the free! La Cu-ca-

(Hum_____)

ra-cha, La Cu-ca-ra-cha, Now a march and now a dance. La Cu-ca-
ra-cha, La Cu-ca-ra-cha, Bring-ing back a mem-o-ry.

# Captain Jinks

Old Song
*Arr.* R. J. N.

2. I joined my corps when twenty one,
Of course, I thought it capital fun
When the enemy came away I'd run,
For I wasn't cut out for the army.
When I left home, mama she cried,
Mama she cried, mama she cried
When I left home, mama she cried,
He's not cut out for the army.

# Old Mac Donald Had A Farm

Old Song
*Arr.*R.J.N.

2: Duck- - -quack-quack.3: Turkey---gobble-gobble. 4: Pig---oink,oink.5. Ford---rattle, rattle.

Each stanza repeats after it has reached this point*, all material of the preceding stanzas between the stars* and*. The fifth stanza in full would be sung thus:"With a rattle-rattle here, etc. With a oink-oink here, etc. With a gobble-gobble here, etc. With a quack-quack here,etc. With a chick-chick here,etc. Old Mac Donald had a farm, E-I-E-I-O."

# Viennese Refrain

Old Viennese Melody
*Arr.* R. J. N.

I seem to al - way hear that sweet re - frain, Re - call - ing

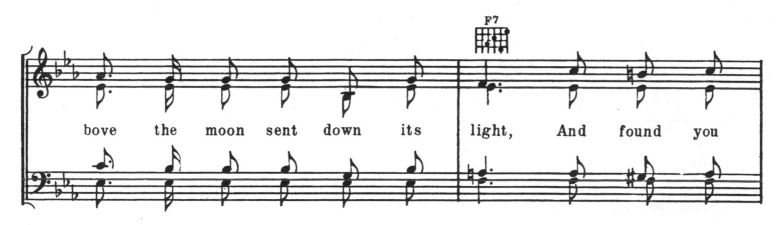

sum - mer skies and wav - ing palms, From high a -

bove the moon sent down its light, And found you

close - ly nes - tled in my arms, And now I nev - er here that mel - o -

# Little Brown Jug

J. E. WINNER
*Arr.* R.J.N.

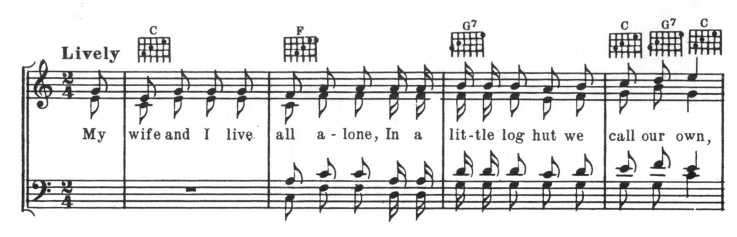

My wife and I live all a-lone, In a lit-tle log hut we call our own,

She loves gin and I love rum, I'll tell you what, we've lots of fun.

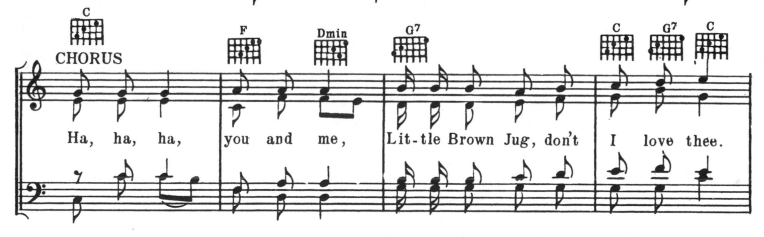

CHORUS

Ha, ha, ha, you and me, Lit-tle Brown Jug, don't I love thee.

Ha, ha, ha, you and me, Lit-tle Brown Jug, don't I love thee.

# Whoopee Ti Yi Yo,
# Git Along Little Dogies

U.S. Western Song
*Arr.* R.J.N.

your mis-for-tune and none of my own, Whoop-ee Ti Yi Yo, git a-long lit-tle do-gies, For you know Wy-o-ming will be your new home.

2. Early in the Spring we round up the dogies;
Mark and brand and bob off their tails;
Round up the horses, load up the churchwagon,
Then throw the dogies upon the long trail.

3. I ain't got no father, I ain't got no mother,
My friends they all left me when first I did roam;
I ain't got no sisters, I ain't got no brothers,
I'm a poor lonesome cowboy and a long way from home

# Home On The Range

U.S. Western Song
*Arr.* R.J.N.

Moderately slow

1. Oh give me a home where the buf-fa-lo roam, Where the deer and the an-te-lope play;— Where sel-dom is heard a dis-

cour - ag - ing word, And the skies are not cloud - y all

CHORUS

day.___ Home, home on the range,___ Where the

deer and the an - te - lope play;___ Where sel - dom is heard a dis -

cour - ag - ing word, And the skies are not cloud - y all day.___

2. Where the air is so pure, the zephyrs so free
   And the breezes so balmy and light;
   I would not exchange my home on the range
   For all of your cities so bright.

# Red River Valley

U. S. Western Song
*Arr.* R. J. N.

2. Won't you think of the valley you're leaving
   Oh, how lonely how sad it will be,
   Oh, think of the fond heart you are breaking,
   And the grief you are causing me to see.

# Nellie Was A Lady

STEPHEN C FOSTER
*Arr.* R.J.N

2. Now I'm unhappy and I'm weeping,
   Can't tote the cottonwood no more,
   Last night when Nellie was asleeping
   Death came aknocking at the door.

3. Down in the meadow 'mong the clover,
   Walk with my Nellie by my side,
   Now all those happy days are over,
   Farewell, my dark Virginny bride.

# Beautiful Dreamer

STEPHEN C. FOSTER
*Arr.* R. J. N.

Beau - ti - ful Dream - er wake un - to me,

Star - light and dew-drops are wait-ing for thee. Oh

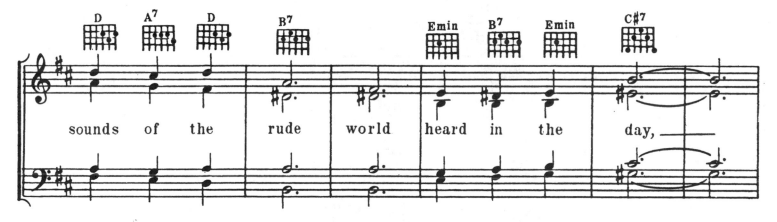

sounds of the rude world heard in the day,

Lull'd by the moon-light have all pass'd a - way. Oh

# Jeanie With The Light Brown Hair

STEPHEN C. FOSTER
*Arr.* R.J.N.

**Slowly**

I dream of Jean - ie with the light brown hair,

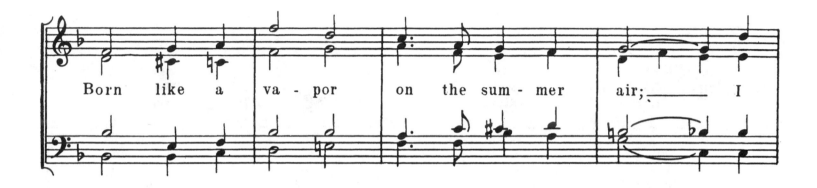

Born like a va - por on the sum - mer air;____ I

see her trip - ping where the bright streams____ play,

Hap - py as the dai - sies that dance on her way.

Ma - ny were the wild__ notes her mer - ry voice would pour,

Ma - ny were the blithe birds that war - bled them o'er;____ I

dream of Jean - ie with the light. brown__ hair,__

Float - ing like a va - por on the soft sum - mer air.

# Old Black Joe

STEPHEN C. FOSTER
*Arr.* R.J.N.

1. Gone are the days__ when my heart was young and gay, (and gay)__

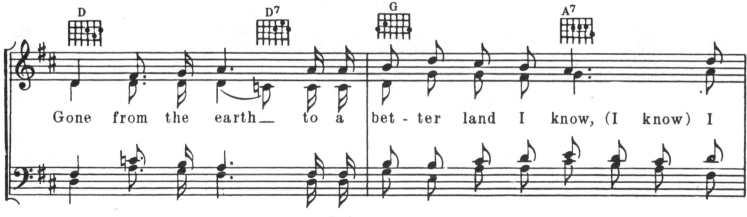

Gone are my friends from the cot-ton fields a - way, (a-way)__

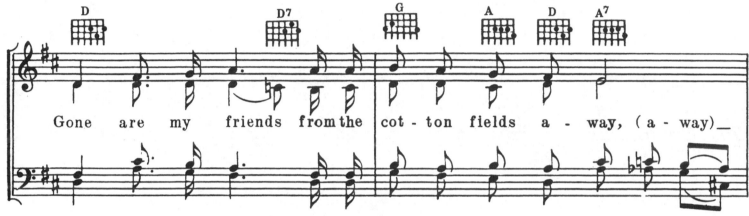

Gone from the earth__ to a bet-ter land I know, (I know) I

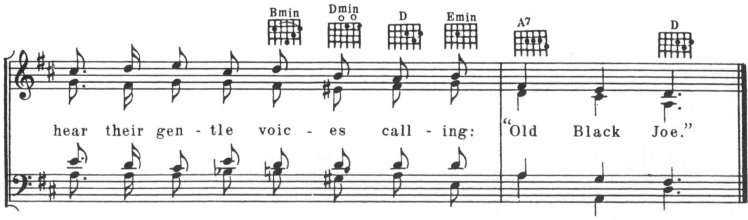

hear their gen - tle voic - es call - ing: "Old Black Joe."

2.

Why do I weep when my heart should feel no pain?
Why do I sigh that my friends come not again?
Grieving for forms now departed long ago,
I hear their gentle voices calling, "Old Black Joe."
CHO.
I'm coming, I'm coming, for my head is bending low,
I hear their gentle voices calling, "Old Black Joe."

3.

Where are the hearts once so happy and so free?
The children so dear that I held upon my knee?
Gone to the shore where my soul had long'd to go,
I hear their gentle voices calling, "Old Black Joe."
CHO.
I'm coming, I'm coming, for my head is bending low,
I hear their gentle voices calling, "Old Black Joe."

# Oh! Susanna

STEPHEN C. FOSTER
*Arr.* R.J.N.

2. I had a dream the other night, when ev'rything was still;
   I tho't I saw Susanna acoming down the hill.
   The buckwheat cake was in her mouth, the tear was in her eye;
   Says I, I'm coming from the South Susanna don't you cry.

CHO: Oh! Susanna, oh, don't you cry for me,
For I'm goin' to Lou'siana with my banjo on my knee.

# When The Corn Is Waving Annie Dear

CHARLES BLAMPHIN
*Arr.* R.J.N.

2. When the corn is waving, Annie dear, our tales of love we'll tell,
   Beside the gentle flowing stream that both our hearts know well.
   Where wild flow'rs in their beauty will scent the ev'ning breeze,
   Oh haste, the stars are peeping and the moon's behind the trees,
   When the corn is waving Annie dear, our tales of love we'll tell,
   Beside the gentle flowing stream that both our hearts know well.

# Comin' Thro' The Rye

Scotch Melody
*Arr.* R. J. N.

2. If a body meets a body, comin' thro' the rye,
   If a body greet a body, need a body frown?

CHO. Ev'ry lassie has her laddie, nane they say ha'e I,
   Yet a' the lads they smile on me, when comin' thru the rye.

# Annie Laurie

Lady JOHN SCOTT
*Arr.* R.J.N.

1. Max - wel - ton's braes are bon-nie, Where ear - ly fa's the dew, And 'twas
there that An - nie Lau - rie Gave me her prom - ise true; Gave
me her prom - ise true, Which ne'er for - got will be, And for
bon - nie An - nie Lau - rie I'd lay me doon and dee.

2. Her brow is like the snowdrift, her throat is like the swan,
   Her face it is the fairest, that e'er the sun shone on;
   That e'er the sun shone on, and dark blue is her e'e,
   And for bonnie Annie Laurie, I'd lay me doon and dee.

3. Like dew on the gowan lying is th' fa' o' her fairy feet,
   And like winds in summer sighing, her voice is low and sweet,
   Her voice is low and sweet, and she's a' the world to me,
   And for bonnie Annie Laurie, I'd lay me doon and dee.

# Long, Long Ago

THOMAS H. BAYLY
*Arr.* R. J. N.

Slowly

1. Tell me the tales that to me were so dear, (so dear) Long, long a-go, (a-go) Long, long a-go, (a-go)

Sing me the songs I de-light-ed to hear, (to hear) Long, long a-go, long a-go. (a-go)

Now you are come all my grief is removed, removed Let me for-get that so long you have roved.

2. Do you remember the path where we met,
Long, long ago, Long, long ago,
Ah, yes, you told me you ne'er would forget,
Long, long ago, long ago,
Then, to all others my smile you preferr'd,
Love when you spoke gave a charm to each word,
Still my heart treasures the praises I heard,
Long, long ago, long ago.

3. Tho' by your kindness my fond hopes were rais'd,
Long, long ago, Long, long ago,
You by more eloquent lips have been prais'd,
Long, long ago, long ago.
But by long absence your truth has been tried,
Still to your accents I listen with pride,
Blest as I was when I sat by your side,
Long, long ago, long ago.

# All Through The Night

Old Welsh Melody
*Arr.* R.J.N.

1. Sleep my child, and peace at-tend thee All through the night;

Guar-dian an-gels God will send thee All through the night;(the night)

Soft the drow-sy hours are creep-ing, Hill and vale in slum-ber steep-ing;

I am lov-ing vi-gil keep-ing All through the night.

2. While the moon her watch is keeping, all through the night;
   While the weary world is sleeping, all through the night,
   O'er thy spirit gently stealing, visions of delight revealing,
   Breathes a pure and holy feeling, all through the night.

# Lullaby

W. A. MOZART
*Arr.* R.J.N.

# Cradle Song

JOHANNES BRAHMS
*Arr. R.J.N.*

**Slowly**

2. So good night go to sleep, angels watch o'er thy sleep,
And while dreaming thou shall see, such a lovely Christmas tree.
Dearest close thy eyes, dream of sweet Paradise,
Dream of angels above, go to sleep now my love.

# For He's A Jolly Good Fellow

Old Song
*Arr.* R.J.N.

2. We won't get home until morning, we won't go home until morning,
   We won't get home until morning, till daylight appear!
   Till daylight appear!
   We won't get home until morning, we won't go home until morning,
   We won't get home until morning, till daylight appear!

# Hallelujah-I'm A Bum

Old Song
Arr. R. J. N.

**Moderately fast**

1. Oh, why don't you work_ like oth - er men do. How the

hell can I work when there's no work to do. Hal - le -

lu - jah I'm a bum,_ Hal - le - lu - jah, bum a - gain. Hal - le -

lu - jah give. a hand out to re - vive us a - gain. Hal - le - gain.

2. Oh, I love my boss and my boss loves me,
   And that is the reason I'm so hungry.

# The Bowery

PERCY GAUNT
*Arr.* R.J.N.

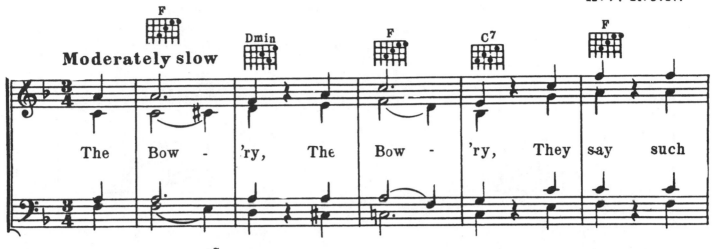

The Bow - 'ry, The Bow - 'ry, They say such

things and they do strange things on the Bow - 'ry, The

Bow - 'ry, I'll nev - er go there an - y - more.

I'll nev - er go there an - y - more.

# Blow The Man Down

SEA CHANTEY
*Arr.* R.J.N.

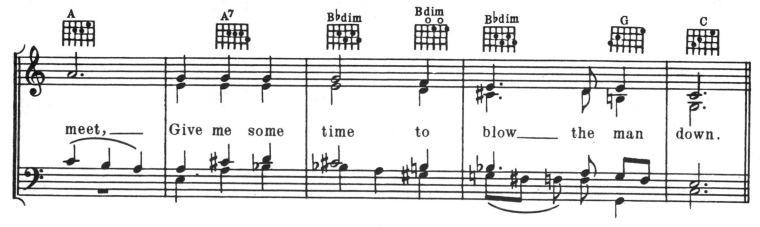

2. Says she to me,"Will you stand a treat?"
Way! Hey! Blow the man down!
Delighted says I, for a charmer so sweet,
Give me some time to blow the man down.

# Down Went Mcginty

JOSEPH FLYNN
*Arr.* R.J.N.

1. Sun-day morn-ing just at nine, Dan Mc- Gin-ty dress'd so fine, Stood a- look-ing at a ver-y high stone wall; When his friend young Pat Mc-Cann, Says, "I'll bet five dol-lars, Dan, I could lift you to the top with-out a fall;" On his

shoul-der he took Dan, Up the lad-der he be-gan, And he

soon com-menc'd to reach up near the top; When Mc - Gin-ty, don't you know, Just to

win the five, let go, Nev - er think-ing just how far he'd have to drop.—

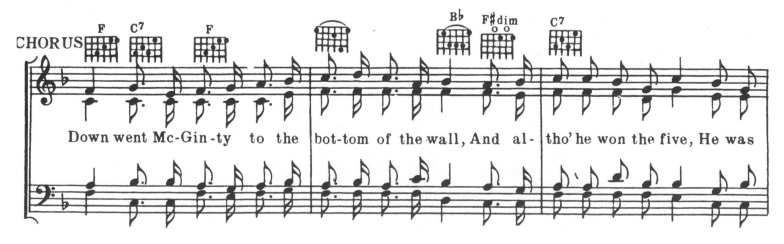

CHORUS Down went Mc-Gin-ty to the bot-tom of the wall, And al- tho' he won the five, He was

more dead than a - live, Sure his ribs and nose and back were broke From get-ting such a fall Dress'd in his best suit of clothes.

2. From the doctor's Mac went home, when they'd fix'd his broken bones,
Just to find he was the father of a child;
So to celebrate it right, his friends he went to invite,
And he soon was drinking whiskey fast and wild;
Then he waddled down the street in his Sunday suit so neat,
Holding up his head as proud as John the Great;
In the sidewalk was a hole to receive a ton of coal,
That McGinty never saw till just too late.

CHO. Down went McGinty to the bottom of the hole,
Then the driver of the cart gave the load of coal a start,
And it took us half an hour to dig McGinty from the coal,
Dress'd in his best suit of clothes.

3. Now McGinty raved and swore, 'bout his clothes he felt so sore,
And an oath he took he'd kill the man or die;
So he tight grabbed his stick and hit the driver a lick,
Then he raised a little shanty on his eye;
Two policeman saw the muss and they soon joined in the fuss,
Then they ran McGinty in for being drunk;
And the Judge says with a smile, "We will keep you for a while
In a cell to sleep upon a prison bunk."

CHO. Down went McGinty to the bottom of the jail,
Where his board would cost him nix, and he stay'd exactly six,
They were big long months McGinty stopp'd for no one went his bail,
Dress'd in his best suit of clothes.

4. Now McGinty thin and pale one fine day got out of jail,
And with joy to see his boy was nearly wild;
To his house he quickly ran to meet his wife Bedaley Ann,
But she skipp'd away and took along the child;
Then he gave up in despair, and he madly pulled his hair,
As he stood one day upon the river shore;
Knowing well he couldn't swim, he did foolishly jump in,
Altho' water he had never took before.

CHO. Down went McGinty to the bottom of the sea,
And he must be very wet, for they haven't found him yet,
But they say his ghost comes 'round the docks before the break of day,
Dress'd in his best suit of clothes.

# I Don't Want To Play In Your Yard

H. W. PETRIE
*Arr.* R.J.N.

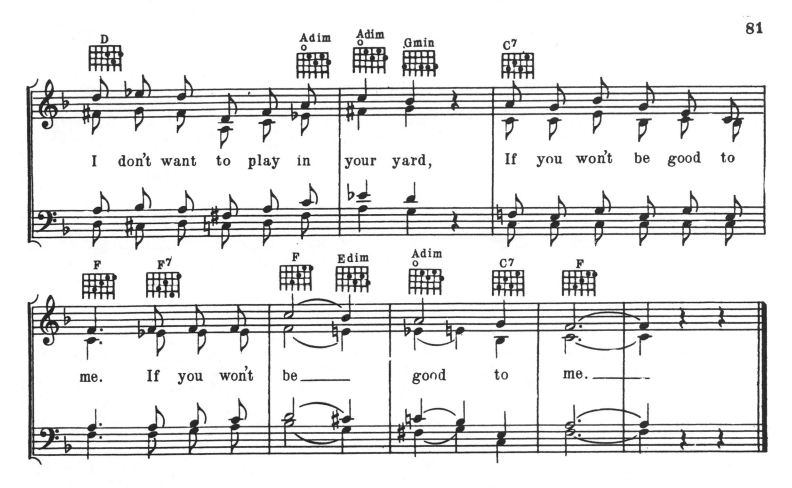

I don't want to play in your yard, If you won't be good to me. If you won't be good to me.

# Daisy Bell

HARRY DACRE
*Arr.* R.J.N.

**In waltz time**

Dai - sy, Dai - sy, Give me your an - swer,

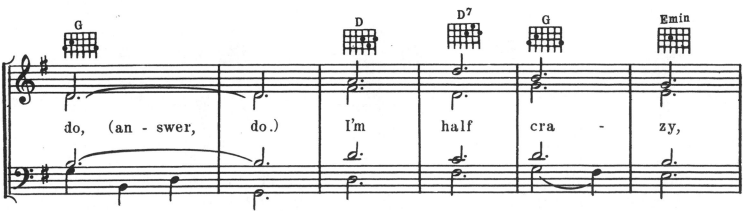

do, (an - swer, do.) I'm half cra - zy,

all for the love of you, (love of you.) It won't be a

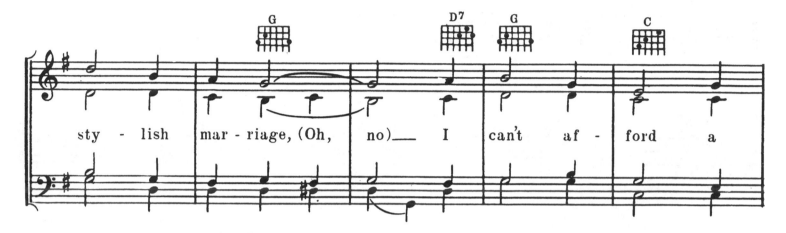

sty - lish mar - riage, (Oh, no)___ I can't af - ford a

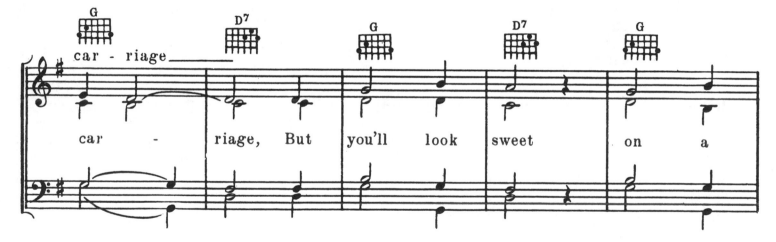

car - riage___ car - riage, But you'll look sweet on a

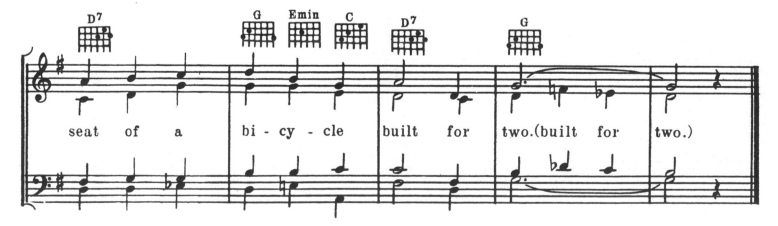

seat of a bi - cy - cle built for two. (built for two.)

# While Strolling Thru The Park One Day
## (In The Merry Month Of May)

ED. HALEY
*Arr.* R.J.N.

# Alouette

French Canadian Folk Song
*Arr.* R. J. N.

1. A - lou-et - te, gen-tile A - lou-et - te, A - lou-et - te, Je te plu-me-rai.
2. A - lou-et - te, gen-tile A - lou-et - te, A - lou-et - te, Je te plu-me-rai.

Je te plu-me-rai la tete, Je te plu-me-rai la tete, Et la tete, Oh!
Je te plu-me-rai la bec, Je te plu-me-rai la bec, Et la bec,
Et la tete,

Et la tete
Et la bec
Et la tete

3. Le nez.  5. Les pattes.
4. Le dos.  6. Le cou.

# Then You'll Remember Me

## From "The Bohemian Girl"

MICHAEL W. BALFE
*Arr* R.J.N.

1. When oth-er lips and oth-er__ hearts, their tales of love shall tell, In lan-guage whose ex-cess__ im-parts, the pow'r they feel so well; There may per-haps in such__ a__ scene, Some rec-o-lec-tion__ be,__ Of

days that have as hap - py___ been, And you'll re - mem - ber___

me, ___ And you'll re - mem - ber, You'll re - mem - ber me.

2. When coldness or deceit shall slight, the beauty now they prize,
And deem it but a faded light, which beams within your eyes;
When hollow hearts shall wear a mask, 'twill break your own to see
In such a moment I but ask, that you'll remember me
That you'll remember, you'll remember me.

# O, Canada

C. LAVALLEE & R.S.WEIR
*Arr.* R.J.N.

1. O Can - a - da! Our home and na - tive land!
2. O Can - a - da! Where pines and ma - ples grow,

True pat - riot love in all thy sons com - mand. With
Great prair - ies love spread and lord - ly riv - ers flow, How

# The Maple Leaf Forever

ALEXANDER MUIR
*Arr.* R.J.N.

1. In days of yore, from Brit-ain's shore, Wolfe the daunt-less he-ro came, Ant plant-ed firm Bri-tan-ia's flag, On Can-a-da's fair do-main; Here may it wave, our boast and pride, And join in love to-geth-er, The

2. At Queens-town Heights, and Lun-dy's Lane, Our brave fa-thers side by side, For free-dom, homes and loved one's dear, Firm-ly stood and no-bly died; And those dear rights which they main-tain'd We swear to yield them nev-er, Our

This - tle, Sham - rock, Rose en - twine The Ma - ple Leaf for - ev - er.
watch - word ev - er - more shall be, The Ma - ple Leaf for - ev - er.

CHORUS

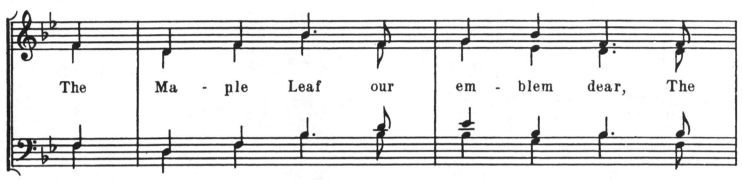

The Ma - ple Leaf our em - blem dear, The

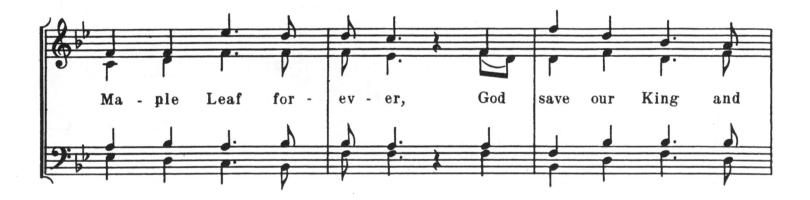

Ma - ple Leaf for - ev - er, God save our King and

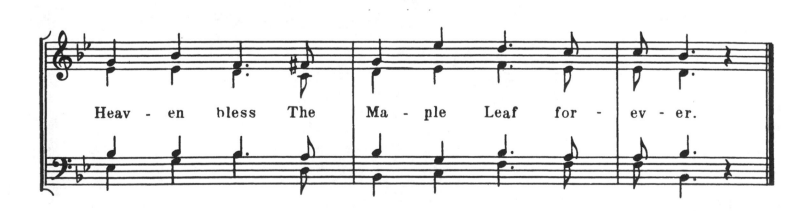

Heav - en bless The Ma - ple Leaf for - ev - er.

# Canadian Boat Song

French Canadian
*Arr.* R.J.N.

# America

SAMUEL F. SMITH
*Arr. R.J.N.*

2. Let music swell the breeze,
   And ring from all the trees,
   Sweet freedom's song,
   Let mortal tongues awake,
   Let all that breathe partake,
   Let rocks their silence break,
   The sound prolong.

3. Our father, God to thee,
   Author of liberty,
   To thee we sing,
   Long may our land be bright,
   With freedom's holy light,
   Protect us by thy might,
   Great God our king.

# The Star-Spangled Banner

FRANCIS SCOTT KEY
*Arr.* R.J.N.

2.

On the shore, dimly seen thro' the mists of the deep,
Where the foe's haughty host in dread silence reposes,
What is that which the breeze oe'r the towering steep,
As it fitfully blows, half conceals half discloses?
Now it catches the gleam of the morning's first beam,
In full glory reflected now shines on the stream,
'Tis the Star-spangled Banner, oh, long may it wave,
O'er the land of the free and the home of the brave!

3.

Oh, thus be it ever when free men shall stand,
Between their loved homes and the wars desolation!
Blest with vict'ry and peace, may the heav'n rescued land,
Praise the pow'r that hath made and preserved us a nation!
Then conquer we must when our cause it is just.
And this be our motto: "In God is our trust!"
And the Star-spangled Banner, in triumph shall wave,
O'er the land of the free and the home of the brave!

# The Battle Cry Of Freedom

GEORGE F. ROOT
*Arr. R.J.N.*

1. Yes we'll ral - ly round the flag boys, we'll ral - ly once a - gain,

Shout - ing the bat - tle cry of free - dom; We will

ral - ly from the hill - side, we'll gath - er from the plain,

Shout - ing the bat - tle cry of free - dom.

2. We will welcome to our number the loyal, true and brave,
   Shouting the battle cry of freedom;
   And altho, they may be poor, not a man shall be a slave,
   Shouting the battle cry of freedom.

3. So we're springing to the call from the East and from the West,
   Shouting the battle cry of freedom;
   And we'll prove a loyal crew for the land we love the best,
   Shouting the battle cry of freedom.

# Battle Hymn Of The Republic

W. STEFFE
*Arr.* R. J. N.

In steady march rhythm

1. Mine eyes have seen the glo - ry of the

com - ing of the Lord; He is

tramp - ling out the vint - age where the

grapes of wrath are stored; He hath

loosed    the    fate - ful    light - ning    of    His

ter - ri - ble swift sword, His    truth is march - ing    on.

CHORUS

Glo - ry, glo - ry! Hal - le -    lu - jah!    Glo - ry, glo - ry! Hal - le -    lu - jah!

Glo - ry, glo - ry! Hal - le -    lu - jah! His    truth is march - ing    on.

2. I have seen Him in the watch-fires of a hundred circling camps;
They have builded Him an altar in the ev'ning dews and damps;
I can read His righteous sentence by the dim and flaring lamps,
His day is marching.

He has sounded forth the trumpet that shall never call retreat;
He is sifting out the hearts of men before His judgment seat;
Oh, be swift my soul, to answer Him! be jubilant my feet!
Our God is marching.

# The Minstrel Boy

Irish Folk Song
*Arr. R.J.N.*

**Rather fast**

1. The min-strel boy___ to the war is gone, In the

ranks of death___ you will find___ him, His

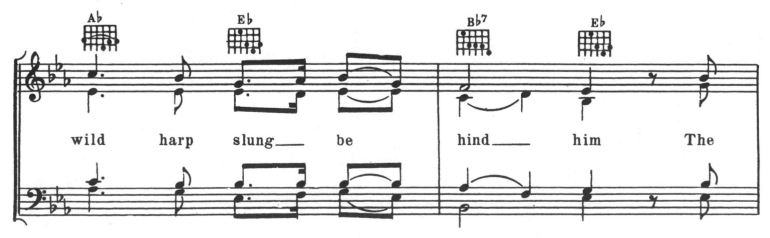

fa-ther's sword___ he hath gird-ed on And his

wild harp slung___ be hind___ him The

land of Song said the war-rior bard "Tho' all the world be-trays thee, One sword at least thy rights shall guard, One faith-ful harp shall praise thee."

2. The minstrel fell but foeman's chain
   Could not bring that proud soul under;
   The harp he loved ne'er hath spoke again,
   For he tore its chords asunder,
   And said "No chain shall sull thee,
   Thou soul of love and bravery,
   Thy songs were made for the poor and free,
   They shall never sound in slav'ry."

# Go Down Moses

Negro Spiritual
Arr. R. J. N.

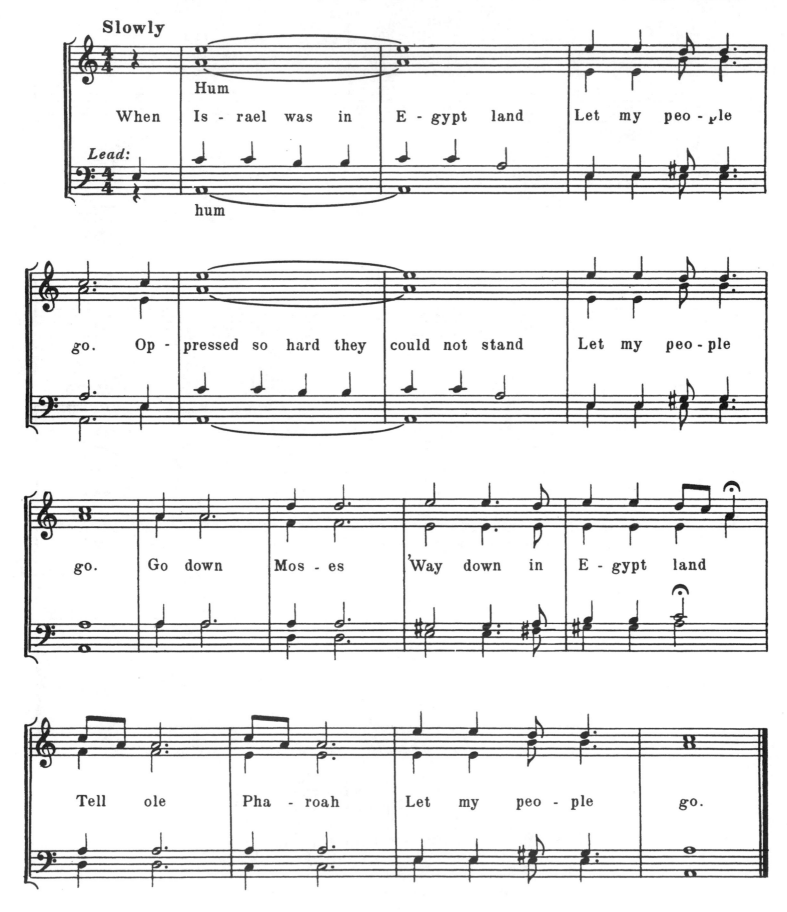

# Nobody Knows The Trouble I've Seen

Negro Spiritual
*Arr.* R.J.N.

# Swing Low Sweet Chariot

Negro Spiritual
*Arr.* R.J.N.

**Moderately slow**

Swing low, sweet char-i-ot,__ Com-in' for to car-ry me home!

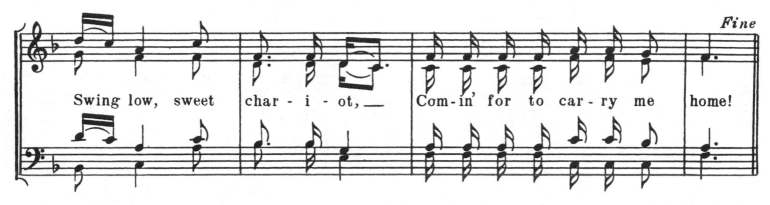

*Fine*

Swing low, sweet char-i-ot,__ Com-in' for to car-ry me home!

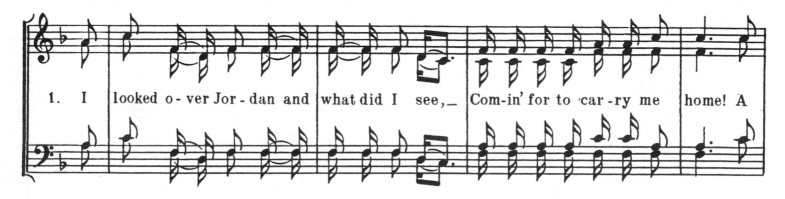

1. I looked o-ver Jor-dan and what did I see,__ Com-in' for to car-ry me home! A

*D.C. al Fine*

band of an-gels com-in' af-ter me,__ Com-in' for to car-ry me home!

2. If you get there before I do,
   Comin' for to carry me home!
   Tell all my friends that I'm acomin' too,
   Comin' for to carry me home!

3. I'm sometimes up an' sometimes down,
   Comin' for to carry me home!
   But still my soul feels heav'nly boun',
   Comin' for to carry me home!

# Oh Freedom

Negro Spiritual
*Arr.* R. J. N.

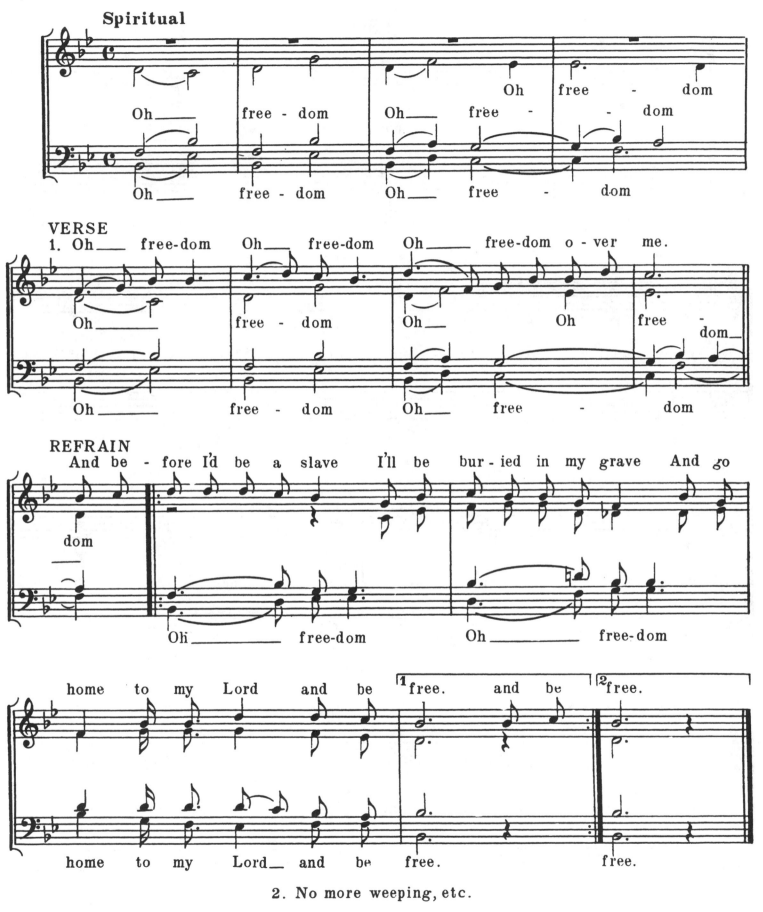

2. No more weeping, etc.

3. There'll be singing, etc.

# Poor Wayfarin' Stranger

Spiritual
*Arr.* R.J.N.

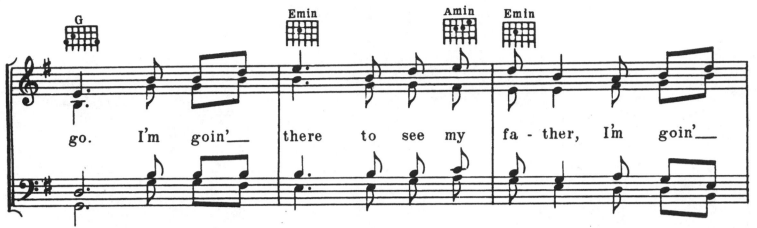

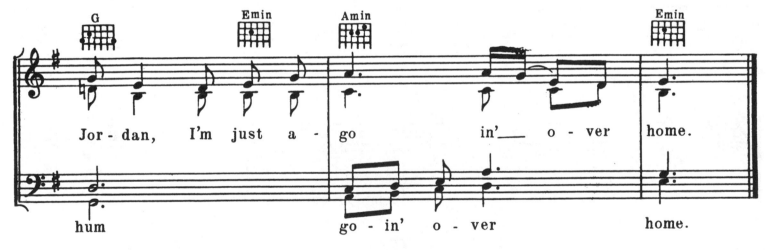

2. I know dark clouds will gather round me,
   I know my way is rough and steep,
   But golden fields lay out before me
   Where God's redeemed no more shall weep.
   I'm going there to see my mother,
   She said she'd meet me when I come,
   I'm just agoing over Jordan,
   I'm just agoing over home.

3. I'll soon be free from ev'ry trial,
   My body sleeps in the old churchyard,
   I'll drop the cross of self-denial
   And enter on my great reward.
   I'm going there to see my Saviour,
   To sing His praise for evermore,
   I'm just agoing over Jordan,
   I'm just agoing over home.

# Deep River

Negro Spiritual
*Arr.* R. J. N.

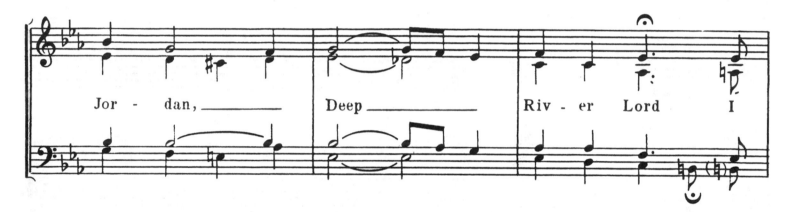

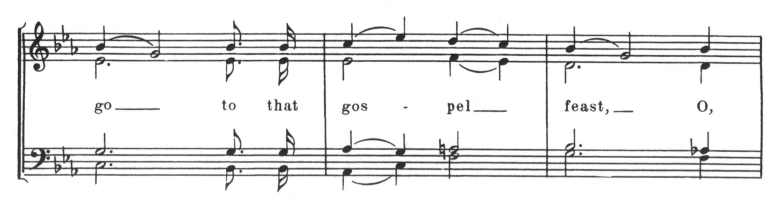

don't you want to go to that prom-ised land, Where all

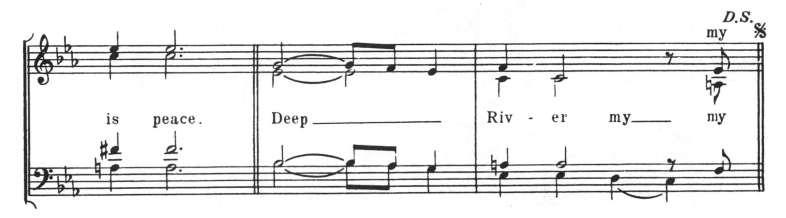

is peace. Deep _____ Riv - er my___ my

D.S. %
my

# The First Noel

Christmas Carol
*Arr.* R.J.N.

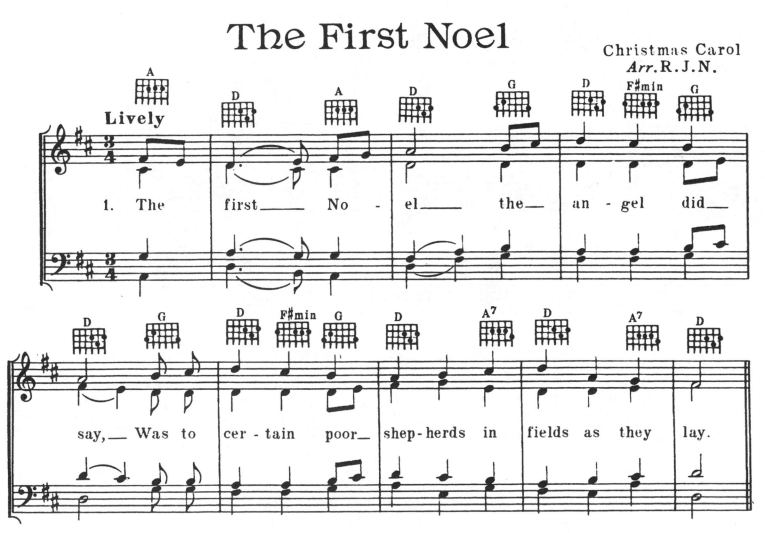

Lively

1. The first___ No - el___ the___ an - gel did___

say,___ Was to cer - tain poor___ shep-herds in fields as they lay.

In __ fields __ where __ they __ lay __ keep - in' their __

sheep, On a cold win - ter's night __ that was __ so deep.

No - el __ No - el No - el __ No - el __

Born is the King __ of __ Is ra - el.

2. They looked above, and there saw a star,
   As it shone in the East but beyond them afar;
   And to the earth it gave forth great light,
   And continued so both day and night.

# Silent Night

FRANZ GRÜBER
*Arr.* R.J.N.

**Slowly**

1. Si - lent night!__ Ho - ly night!__ All is calm, bright (all is bright.) Round yon vir - gin moth - er and child,(and child) Ho - ly in - fant so ten-der and mild,(and mild) Sleep in heav - en - ly peace,__ Sleep__ in heav - en - ly peace.

all is calm, all is bright.

2. Silent night! Holy night!
   Shepherds quake at the sight!
   Glories stream from heaven afar,
   Heav'nly hosts sing Alleluia,
   Christ, the Savior, is born!
   Christ, the Savior, is born!

3. Silent night! Holy night!
   Son of God, love's pure light!
   Radiant beams from Thy Holy face,
   With the dawn of redeeming grace,
   Jesus, Lord, at Thy birth,
   Jesus, Lord, at Thy birth.

# O, Little Town Of Bethlehem

LEWIS H. REDNER
*Arr. R.J.N.*

2. How silently, how silently, the wond'rous gift is giv'n!
   So God imparts to human hearts the blessings of His heav'n.
   No ear may hear His coming, but in this world of sin,
   Where meek souls will receive Him, still The dear Christ enters in.

3. O holy Child of Bethlehem, descend to us we pray;
   Cast out our sin, and enter in, be born in us today.
   We hear the Christmas angels the great glad tiding tell;
   O come to us abide with us, our Lord Emanuel.

# Hark! The Herald Angels Sing

MENDELSSOHN
*Arr.* R.J.N.

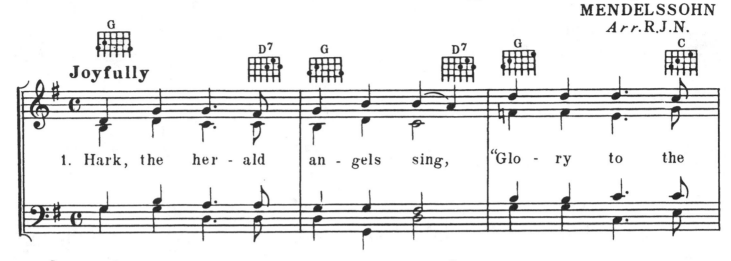

**Joyfully**

1. Hark, the her - ald an - gels sing, "Glo - ry to the

new - born King, Peace on earth and mer - cy mild,

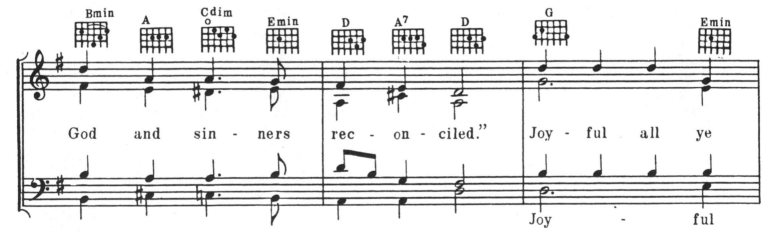

God and sin - ners rec - on - ciled." Joy - ful all ye

Joy - ful

na - tions rise, Join the tri - umph of the skies,

na - tions rise,

With th'an-gel-ic host pro-claim, Christ is born in Beth-le-hem,

Hark, the her-ald an-gels sing, "Glo-ry to the new-born King."

2. Christ by highest Heav'n adored;
   Christ the everlasting Lord;
   Late in time behold Him come,
   Offspring of the favored one,
   Veiled in flesh, the God-head see;
   Hail th' incarnate deity;
   Pleased, as man, with men to dwell,
   Jesus our Immanuel!
   Hark! the herald angels sing
   "Glory to the new-born King."

3. Hail! the Heav'n born Prince of peace!
   Hail! the Son of Righteousness;
   Light and life to all he brings,
   Ris'n with healing in his wings.
   Mild he lays glory by,
   Born that man no more can die.
   Born to raise the Sons of earth,
   Born to give them second birth.
   Hark! the herald angels sing
   "Glory to the new-born King."

# O, Come, All Ye Faithful

J. READING
*Arr.* R.J.N.

Majestically

1. O come all ye faith-ful, Joy-ful and tri-umph-ant, O

2. O sing, chorus of angels, sing in exultation
   Sing all ye citizens of heav'ns giv'n
   Word of the Father now in flesh appearing.

CHO. O come, let us adore Him,
   O come, let us adore Him,
   O come, let us adore Him
   Christ, the Lord.

# Ave Maria

FRANZ SCHUBERT
*Arr.* R.J.N.

A - ve Ma - ri - a! Maid - en

mild O lis - ten to a maid - en's

pray'r. For thou canst hear tho' from the

wild, Thou canst save a - mid de - spair a -

mid _____ de-spair. Safe may we sleep be - neath thy care, Tho'

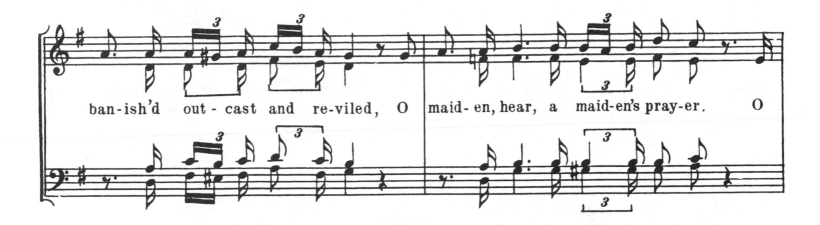

ban-ish'd out - cast and re-viled, O maid-en, hear, a maid-en's pray-er. O

moth - er, hear a sup-pli-ant child. A - ve Mà - ri -

*Optional end*

a, A - ve Mar - ie, Ma - ri - a.

# Death Is A Long, Long Sleep

## 4 Part Round

JOSEPH HAYDN
*Arr.*R.J.N.

*Shows the start of each repetition of the round.

# Mistress Shady
## (2 Part Round)

Traditional
*Arr.* R.J.N.

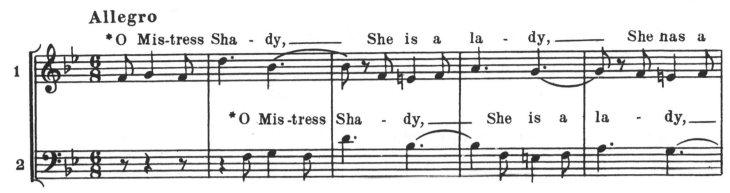

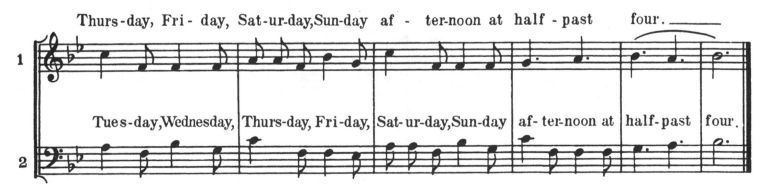

*Shows the start of each part.

# Lovely Evening
## (3 Part Round)

Traditional
*Arr.* R.J.N.

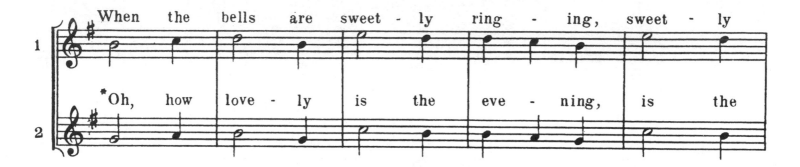

* Shows the start of each part.

# The Bell Doth Toll

## (3 Part Round)

Traditional
*Arr.* R. J. N.

*Shows the start of each part.

# Sing-A-Ling-A-Ling

## (3 Part Round)

Old Song
*Arr,* R. J. N.

*Shows the start of each part.
X substitute any desired name.

# Three Blind Mice
## (4 Part Round)

Traditional
*Arr.* R.J.N.

* Shows the start of each part.

# Row, Row, Row Your Boat

## (4 Part Round)

Traditional
*Arr.* R.J.N.

*Shows the start of each part.

# Scotland's Burning

## (4 Part Round)

Traditional
Arr. R.J.N.

*Show the start of each part.

# She Smiles All The While

(4 Part Round)

Old Song
*Arr.* R.J.N.

*Use any name*

* Shows the start of each part.